Soul
Painting

by

Jocelyn Mosman

inner child press, ltd.

General Information

Soul Painting

Jocelyn Mosman

1st Edition : 2014

Publisher Information
1st Edition : Inner Child Press :
intouch@innerchildpress.com
www.innerchildpress.com

Dedication

Jim and Jennifer Mosman

Jan and William Stein

Ann and Ed Mosman

Jessica, Jon, and Taylor Grondin

Jelene Ballard, Teresa Gazella, and Robert Shaw

Preface

Dear Readers,

Poetry, like life, changes and takes on different meanings and directions as we change and grow. Each of the poems in this book demonstrates that process of change for me. From a young adult's perspective, these poems create a sense of the world I lived in and embraced. Whether it was failed romances or learning to love my body or embracing my role as a powerful woman, each poem is a symbol of that realization.

I could tell you that what you read in the next 100 pages will be encouraging, uplifting, and inspirational. I could also tell you that it will be angsty, depressed, and hopeless. Both are true. This book is about a journey, specifically, my journey, though I hope to share it with all of you. I have found that life is full of beautiful surprises, but also full of challenges. It's full of love, but also heartbreak. Culture, but also ignorance. My hope for this book is that it painstakingly reflects life, from the perspective of a 19-year-old woman.

One thing I expect to be noticed about this poetry book is that it is in 5 parts. I ask that you consider each part to be a stepping-stone within our journey. They are broken, but reassembled, scenes of the life I have been witness to and a part of for the past nearly two decades.

Part 1 is written out of love for the superheroes in my life. It asks to be read with respect, passion, and understanding for the unsung heroes in our everyday lives. From the housewife to the hardworking ex-boyfriend to the strong feminist, I hope that they receive the acknowledgment and accolades that they deserve. One poem that is very dear to me within this part of the book is *Soldier*, which is written for my grandfather, who passed away in 2011. This book is dedicated, in part, to him, for his influence on my life. Through our shared love for verse, I hope for him to be remembered as long as my pens have ink and my paper has blank spaces.

Part 2 is dedicated to Asian forms of poetry, namely the haiku and the sijo. I was blessed to have had a master class with Harvard professor

David McCann in the Korean poetry form of sijo my first semester at Mount Holyoke College. It is a beautiful art form that is generally sung. Perhaps my own sijo lacks that unique beauty found within the Korean language, but keeps the formal amount of syllables per section and is an ironic tribute to the haiku artist, Basho. The rest of the section is written in haiku. *Artist*, a haiku poem written in two parts, asks you to reflect upon the title of this book, *Soul Painting*, and be a witness to the different forms of art that is molded and created and displayed. We, too, like art, ask to be transformed from a blank canvas into something spectacular. My passion for the Japanese haiku was inspired by a dear friend and fellow poet, Dalyn Spurgeon, without whom, I would never have written the haikus you will read in this book.

Part 3 is entitled *Les Papillons*, meaning "the butterflies." Much like this book, butterflies transform throughout their lives. A butterfly is not just beautiful because of the color of its wings, but because of the struggle it goes through from caterpillar to cocoon to butterfly. It is that struggle that I related to, and continue to relate to, throughout my own life. A bit of a personal story belongs with this concept for me. Like other parts of this book, the story is painful both to tell and to read. When I was thirteen, I had a dear friend of mine who was harming herself physically. In order to prevent her from continuing this process, I drew a butterfly on her wrist and asked her not to keep its wings from flying. At the end of that year, she left me a note that read: "Thanks for the butterfly." This part of the book speaks especially to the natural parts of our world, the beauty of struggle, and the success that arises from struggle.

Perhaps my favorite part of the book takes place in Part 4. This part is deeply personal and was, perhaps, the most difficult part to share with you. It is the story of my struggle, my depression, and my darker moments. In a sense, it is my *Black Hole*. The exception to this being my story is the poem *Side Effects*, where I play with the ideas of madness and femininity. From the Victorian Period and earlier, characters such as Ophelia were seen as mad and wildly feminine. I believe that this concept is still present today in how women are treated publicly and privately. This section of the book allowed me to explore the deeper, darker meanings behind my role as a woman and as a warrior fighting my own battles. While it is extremely personal, I hope that in sharing it, you, my dear readers, will find refuge and acceptance within these words. No battle should ever be fought entirely alone.

The final part of this book takes the title, *Soul Painting*. This section is the most artistically inspired within the book. As a poet, I take inspiration from everything. Whether it is a painting, a song, a poem, a sculpture, an animal, or another human being, it has the ability to inspire me profoundly. The first poem within this section is my explanation to *Why I Write*, which is then followed by 6 poems, all beginning with the letter S. To explain the S's, I have a fascination with letters and words and the texture of sounds. Each word has a certain color, and it is my job to paint a picture with the words I have chosen. This section comes from my respect for music, literature, and art. It is a combination of colors, blending and mixing together, to create a final masterpiece of art. Like words in a poem. Like poems in a book. Like people who come and go in our lives and leave us with finger paint on our hearts. That is what this book was created to commemorate.

Please join me in this journey of love, loss, passion, pain, and the human experience, as seen through the eyes of a young woman finding her wings, her paintbrush, her pen, and herself.

Much love,
Jocelyn Mosman

Foreword

"Soul Painting" is the second collection by poet Jocelyn Mosman. 19 years old, Mosman has already been writing for a decade. This collection shows a wide range, from humor to sarcasm, from love to hate. Her poems have an equally wide range – from clever rhyme to an entire section of Haiku, to a section of longer prose.

In "Revolution" Mosman writes "I've scratched full poems/ into my arms hoping/ that one day I'd bleed out/ a verse that rhymed with/ salvation." Then, in "When Superheroes Take Off Their Masks," she completely changes emotions with "…Remember that your love for/ Batman was so freaking annoying/ because I was a Spiderman sort of woman." Poems like the lovely "Turn Me Over" vie for space with "Why I Write", in which Mosman says "I want to write poetry,/ not death certificates/ to ex-lovers and ex-friends".

"Soul Painting" reminds me of a quote from "A Room with a View", when Mr. Beebe says "If Miss Honeychurch ever takes to live as she plays, it will be very exciting both for us and for her." Jocelyn Mosman is our Miss Honeychurch. She is one to watch.

Tobi Cogswell
co-editor and co-publisher
San Pedro River Review

Table of Contents

Table of Contents ... *continued*

Part 3: Les Papillons   37

Part 4: Pushed   45

Table of Contents ... *continued*

"As music is the poetry of sound, so is painting the poetry of sight."

~ James McNeil Whistler

Soul Painting

by

Jocelyn Mosman

inner child press, ltd.

Part 1

Superheroes

"You either die a hero or you live
long enough to see yourself
become the villain."

-Batman

Soul Painting

Superwoman

Tonight, when I look at myself in the mirror,
I see Superwoman.

I see the woman
That prays as much as she slaves away
At her work,
Waiting for the moment when genius
Collides with patience.

Tonight, when I look at myself in the mirror,
I see Superwoman.

But some days, I don't.
Those days I notice the stress lines
Writing poetry onto her countenance,
A message of wisdom and of pain,
The kind of pain that rain does not ever
Wash away by day.
The kind that stays and stays through
Long nights and long days until
Full novels are written on the white pages
Of her flesh.

Tonight, when I look at myself in the mirror,
I see Superwoman.

I see a woman, who knows she's on thin ice,
And enjoys stomping on it,
Just to feel the world open beneath her.

She knows that when her archenemy returns,
His fists will be as thick as the beer on his breath.
And she swears that she can feel it burn
Beneath her feet as she walks on the hot coals
Of his rules, each more cruel than the last.

Soul Painting

Tonight, when I look at myself in the mirror,
I see Superwoman.

But when I don't, I see my future.
I see every gray strand of hair
Twisted into knots only boy scouts could untie,
Wrapped with the thorns of every lie
He ever whispered and every sigh
She ever allowed to escape her fragile lips.

If they were a package, they would be labeled "Handle
With Care,"
But there wasn't much care when he dared
To let his hands talk more than his lips.

Tonight, when I look at myself in the mirror,
I see Superwoman.

I see the multicolor bruises fade into the pigments
Of her pink flesh, fresh
With the tears of another lost dream.

Superwoman dreams.

Tonight, when she leaves him for a new tomorrow,
Drinking down his sorrows with another glass,
She looks into the mirror, and she sees a woman.
Beautiful and proud,
Unable to be too quiet or too loud.

Tonight, when I look at myself in the mirror,
I see Superwoman.

Some nights, she is not so strong.
She wonders if he is the soul mate that he claims
To be, or if he is just a man that she gives pity,
Every time he walks through that door.

4

But some days, she knows that she is on the right path,
That she is on the path towards freedom,
And that his hateful wrath won't stop
Her from being free.

She still racks the aisles of fond memories
Until she finds that the only ones that matter
Are those that scream their stories
From her scars, and the stars never shined
So bright as they do tonight.

Tonight, when I look at myself in the mirror,
I see Superwoman.

A Poem For My Ex

I don't have an O-face.
Scorning the sound
Of your name is more of
My pace,
So I called you Poet
And left the blame
For her eyes to catch
When you fell flat
On your chest
From tripping over
Your own self-hatred.
You told me that you liked circles
So Satan couldn't get you in a corner,
Or maybe it was God who couldn't.
Or maybe, just maybe, it was me who you didn't want
In your corner or on your side.
I tried to be your savior,
But her name was closer
To holy than mine,
And there is a shrine
For her burning in
Our throats,
So we don't say her name.
When I was so in love,
I knew that it was the O
That kept us together
And the Oh no, not again
That would keep us apart.
You have been an
Arson away from
Burning down bridges
That led to safety,
And this is on the daily.
My bridges were

Matchsticks
And you set them
Aflame.
I knew the cycle better than most.
But I didn't ever think
That it would end.
The fame of your name
Became infinitely round,
And no matter which way I looked,
You were always surrounding me.
We were intertwined, impossibly.
I was always trying to fit into your circle
Of friends,
Always older,
Always wiser,
Always able to get more drunk.
But, I can't hold my liquor.
The rim of the bottle
And the rim of the cup
Remind me of always
Skating on the outside of your
Inner circle.
When you told me that
A rose by any other name
Would smell as sweet,
I wanted to be the rose
That you didn't cheat on.
And when dawn came,
You made me dizzy
With your hypnotism,
Eyes circling around my
Full moon chest,
Like the rest of me
Was slipping away
To another long day.
My pleasure was your desire.
It reminded me of the tires

Soul Painting

On her jeep that
Drove you away from me.
So I wrote this poem
For our one day
Spouses and children,
Because they won't understand
What we've been through.
It's the shape of
Every teardrop
That comes from the O
In the middle of your name.
Without that O,
You are incomplete.
You turn from Poet to Pet,
And from Tom to
The trademark I haven't
Ever met because
The man I knew wouldn't
Trade me for anything.
You never knew
The bluebonnets in my
Eyes were blooming for you
Because you preferred her
Tiger Lilies growling at you
Protectively.
And I wanted to
Read the scars on her back
Like Braille.
I was too blind to see
Through the evidence.
But you were too fast of a flyer
For me to notice
What a liar could do to
A little fire's heart.
I don't have an O-face,
I just have a face
Because, without that O,

We are incomplete.
Without that O,
We never would have
Learned the words
"Orgasm" or
"Oblivious"
Or "Oxygen."
You told me once,
Through naked breath,
That I had to need you
Like I needed oxygen.
We could've climbed Olympus
Together because we were
Champions of our own omnipotence.
We were gods of our existence,
But I O.D.'ed on the Oxygen Depletion
Of a relationship that never knew
Eternity or everlasting.
Our O's were cut in half,
Split like two U-turns
And driven in opposite directions,
Because opposites don't always attract.
They attack the truth that
We can never be together.
We can never cheat or run away
Or steal each other's hearts again.
Because this is about us,
The "us" that existed once
And the "us" that will never, ever exist again.

Soldier
for Grandpa

I wasn't there that day.
I was thousands of miles away
And trying to attend school
Like a soldier without a cause.
I got the phone call
And it wounded me
Like a bullet to the chest,
My mother's cracked voice
On the other end:
"Tell Grandpa you love him,
Baby, he can hear you."
He'd been comatose for days,
So they said later,
And I was not ready
For my last few words
To the man who was
A thousand miles away,
Lying in a hospital bed,
I wish I could've talked
The dead out of him
In my hushed, cracked voice,
But I was a soldier without a cause
And he was on life support
With my voice as the only goodbye
I could manage.
"I love you, stay strong," I urged,
But my heart was pounding
Like grenades surging
With adrenaline.
I wasn't there that day,
When Philadelphia skies
Cried, sobbing onto earth,
And in sunny Texas,

I was a Pennsylvania reflection.
My eyes were cloudy
With a chance of pain
That would write itself into poetry
Every time I saw his face.
Every time I said his name.
I wanted to be a reflection
Of the man I knew,
A warrior of written word.
January 25th marked the day,
And I had nothing left to say,
When I heard my mother
On the phone,
"He's gone."
I knew the battle was over,
But it felt like pulling the plug
Took the life out of my family,
And my heart keeps beating
Like drums of war,
But it's beating out a cause,
And every subordinate clause
Is a broken promise.
But his silence on the phone
The day I said goodbye
Rang in my ears like gunshots
Singing "Poet, write me in Paradise."
I'm a warrior with a cause.
My cause is him.
I wasn't there that day.
I was a thousand miles away
And I had nothing to say,
But "I love you, stay strong.
I've been writing to you all along."

The Question of Feminism

Feminism is not the trademark
Of sexy women
Or femme lesbians
Or man-haters
Or civil rights movements
Full of piety.
She's not the fool of society
And she doesn't write perfect poetry.
She knows how to look in the mirror,
And see a warrior instead
Of an inferior woman.
Feminism has a name,
And she goes by Wonder Woman.
The thunder in her thighs
Make men sigh, and she
Turns the other way.
She doesn't let me wear
Skimpy clothing on bleak
Winter mornings
Or heels and hoodies in
The evenings,
Because feminism's got standards.
She has walked that thin line
Between masochism
And perfectionism.
She understands bondage
And BDSM like a sex goddess.
She burlesque dances
Like a diva,
But she doesn't crawl
In and out of her porcelain skin
Like a doll.
She is made from anguish,

Not from sitting, looking pretty,
Waiting for a lover.
She doesn't need a cover story
To get up and leave.
Feminism has a question for you.
When it is freezing outside
And you offer her your coat,
Will you do it to share the warmth?
Or will you do it
To show that feminism is weaker than you
On cold evenings
In empty parking lots?
The red and blue lights flash
Like photographs
In her eyes when guys the size
Of policemen come to arrest the man
Who committed murder
Of the body,
And of the soul.
Can a feminist be a feminist
If she isn't whole?
Or is Holy a state of being?
Of seeing eye to eye
With the patriarchy of
Religion and the matriarchy
Of raising babies and cooking?
Feminism wasn't ever much of a chef.
Or a baker.
She is a maker of beliefs,
A philosopher hidden beneath
The "proper feminine attire".
But when she pulls her skirt up,
Snuggling tight against her legs,
And wears a see-through shirt
To show what it means
To not be ashamed of the body

Soul Painting

God gave her,
I wonder if feminism loves herself
Or if she calls herself names
Like a slut or a prude?
Is it still considered rude
To be bullied by your own
Conscience?
The constancy of questioning
Of feminism makes her feel
Like she's on the witness stand
At her trial.
She has been filed away for centuries
While women wait for
Legitimacy to become
Reality.
Is feminism a way to be
The fool of society,
Or a way to go against the crowd?
Feminism isn't loud.
She doesn't protest the mainstream.
Feminism is patient,
Even in oppression,
She does not cry.
And I don't know why,
But when I put on my clothes
And jewelry
And step into my skin,
Made uniquely for me,
I witness how nature feels
Against my breasts.
And I want to know if
I am a feminist.
If I am a Wonder Woman made
To trade my body for nothing,
My soul for star stuff.
If I can begin to walk

In my own shoes and feel
The wriggling of my toes against
A universe set against me
And still call it home.
If I can look at a piece of glass,
And see a miracle instead of
A mess-up.
I have a question for feminism.
Are you accepting applications?
Because I'm interested
In joining your fight
Toward a better future.
We are a brigade of women
Holding a quiet confidence
Through time.
It is not a crime to speak the truth.
My name is Wonder Woman.

Revolution

There's a war zone
In my chest
And it keeps getting ripped
Apart by
Nicotine- age
Bad habits
And falling down
Rabbit holes
Into relationships
That leave me in wonder.
Landing me
In a mess of chess sets
And red blood
Versus white skin.
I want to sacrifice my
One-liners to the muse,
Feel myself fall deep down
Into the depression blues,
Toppling over the Jenga blocks
I used to consider my foundation.
There will always be blood
On the floor,
As I push my way through
The flood of red.
Did you know salmon beat themselves
Bloody against the current
To find true love,
But women make themselves
Bleed once a month
And are grateful there's
No child inside of them?
I wait for blood

To fall from my uterus
Every time we screw,
But I'm stuck
In the waiting for my period,
Waiting for my body to
Extract your seed
To a new world
And plant a tree
Outside of me,
In another woman,
Because no man
Could fall in love
With a girl like me
And not tear down my wall,
Not shed blood and tears
Like all the hidden fears
In my less than bullet proof
Vest.
There's a war zone in my chest and
I bled for days when I prayed
For a revolution in my blood stream
Scratching my skin with
Red letters: "I'm fine."
It was too easy to lie to the masses
Than take the low blow passes
At my insecurities.
I've scratched full poems
Into my arms hoping
That one day I'd bleed out
A verse that rhymed with
Salvation.
I'm just the infection
Spreading through my blood cells,
Toppling empires of self-loving
And creating chaos in
The self-loathing.

Soul Painting

I know what it means to burn,
How hot it must get for flesh
To turn to ash.
I've smoked my way through
Living, hoping that
My war zone of my chest
Is a black liver,
Two smoky lungs,
And a heart with a chain link
Fence surrounding it
And a sign that says:
Beware of dog- she's a real bitch.
My heart is an animal,
That's why my ribs are her cages.
I can't let her loose because
I've created an arsenal of insults
Just in case I needed to fire
At anyone close by.
I wanted to change history,
But what can a nineteen year old
Dictator of a nation with
The population of 1 do
For a world set against loving?
You say you want a revolution,
So watch me burn the bridges
And walk away.

Jocelyn Mosman

Talk Nerdy to Me

I am a huge nerd.
Like, I think you
Are copper and tellurium,
Because you are CuTe
To me.
No, really, my vocabulary
Is as wide as the Atlantic,
And as deep as this poem
Can possibly be.
My favorite word
Is pulchritudinous,
Which, despite its sound,
Means physically attractive.
My other favorite word
Is invincible.
Unable to be beaten down,
Like your libido on a rampage.
Talk nerdy to me.
I am indefatigable
When it comes to poetry,
But I want words to move
Themselves into
Arabesques and pliés.
I want to watch them
Masquerade into stories,
Serenade lovers' ears
With their sunlight sonatas,
Because music
Shouldn't just be played
At moonlight.
Talk nerdy to me.
I want to find chemistry
Between two people,

Soul Painting

And make a bond
Out of separate elements.
Mixing drinks
And mixing genders
Makes chemistry easy.
Talk nerdy to me,
And I'll let you be
Tangent to my curves,
Finding the area below
As attractive as
Einstein found
$E=MC^2$.
Eloping always equals
More children,
Squared.
Talk nerdy to me,
And if you look
For my square root,
I'll be rooted
In the grounds
Of law,
Digging deep
Below the surface.
I want to be
An archaeologist
Searching the bones
In your rib cage
That's locking in
Birds with broken feathers
To keep them safe
From rainy nights.
But I am crying out
Angelou and Auden.
Talk nerdy to me because
I want to understand
That the fire in me

Is burning up
The ice.
My melting point
Is your touch.
My boiling point
Is poetry,
See which one
Makes me hotter.
Talk nerdy to me,
And I'll teach you
The difference between
Chemistry and poetry.
Life is elements of
Science and literary devices.
It's a yoga mat rolled up
Because nerds don't meditate
Imitating a tree,
They meditate watching one,
Arms wide,
Neck high,
Reaching for the sky.
Embrace nature.
I'll be reading Shakespeare
And waiting.
Talk nerdy to me.
Henry the eighth is searching
For a muse of fire,
And I'm burning
To be her.
I want to listen
To Beatles music,
Discuss DNA,
And hold your hand
Like a seashell,
Echoing your heart.
I want you to talk nerdy,

Soul Painting

And I'll teach you
About how one plus one
Makes two,
Unless it makes three.
How math isn't poetry,
And life doesn't always
Fit in a calculator.
But I want to count
The digits on your
Fingers and toes
And know that
We will be making
Footprints in the sand
And fingerprints
In the heart.
Let's Van Gogh
Our way through
Time and space,
Like the Doctor.
I want to be nerdy with you.
Let's make our grand total
The sum of good memories
And of bad goodbyes.
Divide the deciding factors
Between us,
And make a difference
In this world.
Be nerdy with me, love,
Only then will your
Basilisk find a safe home
In my chamber of secrets.
Talk nerdy to me.

Jocelyn Mosman

When Superheroes Take Off Their Masks

It's been seven months,
And I still think about you.
I still change Facebook accounts
So I can see if you are still smiling
In your profile picture,
Or if your new girlfriend
Makes you happier
Than I did when I was
The girl occupying your left
Side of the photo.
It's been seven months,
And I can still smell your
Cologne from 2,000 miles away,
Remember that your love for
Batman was so freaking annoying
Because I was a Spiderman sort of woman.
I remember when it didn't matter
Which superhero was better
Because you were the only super
Heroic man I needed in my life.
And I feel lucky to have seen that side
Of you,
The Tommy D side of your
Nerdy Doctor Who-loving addictions.
The Assassin's Creed tattoo
On your arm and your white lab coat
Of a costume were only part,
But I know you had super powers
Far greater than Optometrist.
I witnessed in my year and a half
Of being in your life
The promise you had in your heart.
It's been seven months,

Soul Painting

And I can't seem to get you out of my head,
And I can't seem to forget the words you said
To me when I was lonely,
The good morning texts,
The stolen kisses,
The fighting with the missus,
But I knew you better.
I knew that your battle wasn't between
Me and you.
I was not your Kryptonite or your Joker.
You were not Batman,
But you were a juggler.
In 18 months, I discovered that
You balanced your family,
Your school, your work, your girlfriend
Like spinning plates,
Keeping everything in check,
And wondering where your paycheck went
Every time you had to pay bills.
It's been seven months,
And I hope that you're one plate lighter,
One part less preoccupied with being busy
And one part more interested in living.
You were a soldier fighting PTSD with
Your liver,
Because alcohol and late night fights
Where we talked about your anger
Only made you ask me if
Your grandfather would be proud
Of the man you'd become.
It's been seven months,
And we have not spoken in four.
But I still check on you
In my quiet little way because
Loving a superhero isn't easy
To give up.

So, I don't let you go.
I don't care how caught up
In the web of lies and of
Imperfect goodbyes I get,
Because it's been seven months,
And I kissed you on the cheek
When I left you,
Another lie piercing through me
As I hugged you.
It was your birthday the other day,
And at 12:04 because Facebook wouldn't let me
Message you at midnight,
I wished you a happy 24th birthday.
And I know, it's been seven months,
And we have not spoken in four,
But I know you read that message.
I cannot believe that it's been 2 years since we met,
But your birthday gave me a chance
And I took the opportunity
To wear the Spiderman shirt you gave me,
Read over our old messages like
Photographs of two people entirely foreign
To me now,
And pretend to understand
How I still think of you when we were marked
With fights and cuss words and low blows,
But I do still think of you.
It's been seven months, and I'm ready
To be the girl who walks away from
The adrenaline junkie superhero,
From the Risk champion,
Sci-Fi loving Geek.
I know you aren't perfect,
But even after seven months,
I haven't forgotten that my War Doctor
Is just a man who is finding love

Soul Painting

2,000 miles away
With a woman who will always be
Better for him than me.
It's been seven months,
And I'm sorry,
Not for loving you,
Not for letting you go,
But for never telling you
To put down the spinning plates,
Take off the mask,
And just be Tommy for a while.
Because after seven months,
I know,
You are enough.

Part 2

Asian Mosaics

"Do not seek to follow
in the footsteps of the wise.
Seek what they sought."

-Basho

Soul Painting

Artist

I. The Painter

He is Picasso
And I am his abstract art,
Bending at his will,

Stained glass window heart
My multi-colored soul melts
In his rainbow craft.

His kiss is the paint,
My white breasts are his canvas:
Black and blue designs.

Skin is the paintbrush
Stroking his flesh against mine,
He dips in for more.

My broken façade
Lacks structure in countenance
Jigsaw shaped outline.

Polygram structure,
His passion was in cubism,
Mine in softer forms.

My flesh is canvas,
His paintings permanently
Displayed on my soul.

Haikus on Commercials

You can come to me
Where you can have it your way
All day and all night.

Supersize my thighs
With your sweet tooth mcflurry
Mmm I'm lovin' it.

I wish I could pay
Five dollars for my boyfriend
To have a foot long.

I want my skin clear
Like Jennifer Aniston
That sexy cougar!

I remember when
I was pepperoni faced
Papa John's pre-teen.

Hair is so silky
Girls tie knots in it as proof
Beat that Rapunzel!

Poor injured duckling
Thank god for insurance claims
Aflac! Quack! Aflac!

When we screw tonight,
I'll think of your fresh produce
And your rollback price.

Haikus for My Poets

My pen and your tongue
Have more in common than thought
Both break hearts all night.

You make my heart Twitch
When your fingers comb my hair,
Love is in the air.

You are beautiful
Like a pink summer sunset
Glowing in my heart.

Haiku my heart, Mute
You are my Charlie Chaplin
White face, quiet soul.

Fishnets and corsets
A fire's been burning in me
Burlesque dancer, breathe!

Caged bird in my ribs
Has been singing out my songs
Broken windpipes play.

Sparrows sing away
Bound by chains of gravity,
The chained bird still sings.

Bluebirds cannot see
The color of naked tears,
They are blind to blue.

Had Basho Written A Sijo

Lily pad on water's surface,

     Sits serenely without ripple,

Blossoming, its petals open,

     Gleaming in the sun, all quiet below.

A frog leaps onto the lily pad,

     And soaking wet floats downstream.

Haikus for My Family

My mother is rose
Flowers and colored glasses
Blossoming each day.

Telling me stories
Of bunnies after bath time,
Mom released tangles.

I watch raindrops race
Down wet car windows and think
I love my sister.

My brain is phone lines
Reaching long distance for you
Needing connections.

My bones have been small
Created for the purpose
To build love on land.

When I see myself
Distorted in rain puddles
Nature makes me strong.

I want to peel back
Your Adam's apple and call
Cardboard voice box "Home."

Haikus for My Ex-Lovers

Your icy touch burns
A lantern in my old soul
Japanese faith floats.

The gold wedding band
Circling around your finger
Dissipates like smoke.

Track marks on my arms
From shooting up convictions
I loved you too much.

My shooting star burns
Scorching letters of your name
In my black hole heart.

When your fists bruise me,
I consider leaving you,
Your kiss is my cure.

You were my poison
Nitroglycerin laced lips
My heart went boom boom.

Painting with pastels
My pink blush met his blue eyes
Yellow dress canvas.

You're breaking records
Like Michael Phelps and 8 tracks,
Your waves drown my love.

Artist

II. The Sculptor

He's Alexandros,
Etching my back with his kiss,
I'm his pristine Muse.

He molded my skin
Like marble in his expert hands,
Masterpiece of flesh.

He chips away lies,
Chiseling down my rough flaws,
Smooth as a goddess.

He called me Venus,
His goddess of affection,
Carved from purest love.

My hourglass waist,
Engraved with his initials,
Reminder of time

O virginity,
An inspiration to men,
Forever made chaste,

I am still his Muse
Erato turned to Clio
Love yields history.

Soul Painting

Part 3

Les Papillons

"Love is like a butterfly, beautiful and delicate…
If you truly care for it, you'll do whatever
you can to make it happy,
even if that means letting it go."

-Scott Pemberton

Soul Painting

Butterflies

Butterflies drawn on my pale wrist

A thin red line is the stop sign

To the truth, drawing the mess that is me

From the wrinkled creases of the Red Sea,

And I feel like Moses and Satan,

Parting the waters with my staff,

Slaughtering a butterfly with a nervous laugh.

The wings fly away, as I try not to cry

At the ephemeral pain that is

The butterfly calling my name.

I'm frantic to live, desperate to kill,

A desperado instilled with duality

Of love and hate, until I create

A new butterfly, permanent and full of light,

Granting me guidance through her flight,

Granting me peace through the night,

Granting me strength at her sight.

She carries my soul to new love.

Turn Me Over

Turn me over like

A dried leaf,

Count my veins

As forgotten dreams.

I escaped

From branches,

Forming droplets of

New beginnings.

I am hues of change.

Family Tree

Shake my branches,

Carve your name

Into my exterior,

Sit under my blanket

Of green shade.

Dig deep down

And find my roots.

This is the story

Of my family tree.

Sing, gentle breeze,

Rustle my falling fruit,

I will stand strong and true,

Through winter and spring.

Watch me grow anew.

Tout J'ai Besoin

Je voudrais les bises,
Les souhaites d'une fille
Je veux un amour si fort
Car mon costume est brillant
À ton touché.

Tes bises me font pleine
D'amour et vide de colère
Car ton amour est tout j'ai besoin.

~ * ~

Translation

~ * ~

All I Need

I want kisses,
The wishes of a girl
I want a love so strong
Because my disguise is glistening
At your touch.

Your kisses make me full
Of love and empty of hate
Because your love is all I need.

Mime

Do you see me?

She asked nervously,

Can you feel my touch?

The face in the mirror

Was silent.

A mime of the past.

~ * ~

I Wrote My Heart

I wrote my heart

Into the page,

Sunk it deep down

Between the lines,

And prayed that

No one would be able

To dig it out or

Rip it up.

Bus B43

Our near empty bus to nowhere,
I noticed them.
Her purple balloon treasure
Sat next to smelly blue seats,
His red jacket warmed frostbitten arms.
She tied tangled hair with pink ribbons,
Reverting back to a childhood mentality,
While he was twitching to silent metal music--
The trees were his violins, and aluminum cans
Were his cellos and drums and basses,
Clanging like cymbals with his jerking motions.
They live off the brutality and kindness of nature.
The leaves were rustling outside like red heartbeats,
Dropping in the autumn wind as we passed by,
Reminded them of the flat-lining summer heat.
His blue dingy bike and paper bag
Left scuff marks on vomit-colored flooring.
Her black backpack ripped at the seams
Matched the ripping seat cover next to her.
Both held bits of brown comfort:
Their cardboard kingdoms,
Filled with rat-infested blankets
And garbage can trophies.
Her dirt smudged chin and
His snaggle-toothed grin,
Both knew that goose bumps
Turned contagious
With colder weather
And shabbier shelters.
A man and a woman, unrelated,
And me.
We were the trio
On Pioneer Valley Transit Authority
Bus B43.

Part 4

Pushed

"Your pain is the breaking
of the shell that encloses
your understanding."

-Kahlil Gibran

Soul Painting

Jocelyn Mosman

Push Me

Push me. Some days I need a little push. And your hands, like my father's, put pressure on my back, push, swing, push, swing, and I resort back to the childhood slingshot landing my stone heart between two love birds. The creases on your aged palms match the laugh lines on my grandfather's face the day before he died, and maybe I wanted to hide that insecurity from you until I was ready to reveal the novels etched onto my skin like ivory, but I want you to read that story now and remember the why I bow my head when I pray to gods I don't even believe in and the how I sit in a church pew still and let the chills of a faith I refuse to admit run down my spine and still cross myself with the words "I'm fine." I need you to push me a little harder, past the starter kit for drugs and booze and sex, and I want you to rock me like a baby in your arms when I'm too drunk to see the stars. The moon is the reflection of the scars located on my right shoulder blade after having stayed a trophy for too long. The thing about trophies... They tarnish. Too many men have pushed me. They've told me I'm beautiful, like I've never heard the words before, but, they fester like a sore infecting every inch of my body. Maybe if they'd stop telling me lies and start telling me truths then we'd start breathing rather than sighing. Push me past the point where I can take your liquor thick on my tongue, nauseating me, push me past the point where when you pull your hand back I prepare for the hit, push me past the point where I get sick of all your bullshhhhh.... Push me like a child on a swing. Push, swing, push, swing. And I'll

47

sing you lullabies in my drunken cradle. Using an empty bottle of beer as the last teardrop that fell for the pain of having to look into a mirror of the criminally insane. My eyes are growing darker, and my soul keeps rocking, rocking, rocking like a baby, crying in the cradle of my cemetery arms. A mother who self harms and a daughter waiting for the charms of a father who pushed too far. Push, swing, push, swing. Can you feel the sting of fresh blood on concrete? Push me. Push me against the wall until I feel your hot breath against my ears, and that searing pain and pleasure shoot through my body like a cannon. Kiss me like it will be your last, and when you get past the point of enjoying me, push me to the next man. I ran to your abuse in the end because Stockholm became the prescription drugs I was overdosing on. Push me to create thin white lines of powder that separates life from death and push me to the edge. Wait for the liquor to take hold of the medication and wait for the sensation of a drug addict and an alcoholic to mix in the bloodstream of a poet and an artist. The monsters under my eyes are throwing parties and I can trace the track marks creating a trail to my heart. Push me. Push me to insanity; push me to the brink of pain. Push me. I feel your rough hands behind me, putting pressure on my back. Push, swing, push, swing. Push me. Until I shatter like a broken bottle in the night. Push me.

D

The dark alleyways of "D" led us down
This tricky path between good and evil
(But I don't think it could be that simple).

It was you and me, since the eighth grade,
And together we made a mess of middle school,
Leaving a trail behind us...

We wrote "D" over and over until it sounded
More truthful than "H."
"Happiness" felt like a curse word in my crooked mouth,
And you only knew frowns (no smiles for us).

We traveled like whores, selling
Ourselves short of self-restraint, and
I knew even then that you were my
(Cursed, hated, rotten) Metallic Monster.

I carried you with me to create designs
Of "D" on white canvas,
Transforming the white into red, red paint.

You got me through the hard days,
(And just like bad sex) you were a reminder
Of my failure and "D."

I met an Angel freshman year,
(You called her a Devil) and
She cut the strings attaching
You to my existence.

I knew with her on my side, I could be free,
But parasites like you don't give up easily,
Not without a fight (to the death).

Soul Painting

I tried breaking you,
But you broke my will.

I tried throwing you away,
But gravity pulled us back together.

I've seen what an addiction can do:
It's written on my body (like pieces of art).

Our creations are the evidence of
The dark alleyways we traveled
So long ago, digging our way down
To the dark pit (of self-pity).

I couldn't cover you up,
My makeup was too yellow,
And you made me feel like a freak,
(Long sleeves, dark circles, red lipstick).

They called "D" a plea for attention;
I called you "Box Cutter"
But I was cutting outside the box.

Couldn't they see, (Why couldn't they see?)
I was falling apart, creating a
Blood bath in dark alleyways,
Just you and me, me and you…

Depression creating my monsters,
Digging deep down (in my darkest holes),
And spilling out around my rough edges
Like red war paint.

Down

My underwear was
Around my ankles,
When you taught me
How to be vulnerable.
I was the girl next door
You scored a
One night stand with
Because I couldn't
Stand looking up to you,
Like my oppression
Was an invitation
For the sensation
Of you going
Down on me.
I make good pillow talk
And let you walk
Right over me
Because being free
Is overrated
When baited breath
And handcuffs are more of
What you want to see
Me wearing.
But just because
You drench me
With your daring kisses
Doesn't mean
I'm not gasping for air
When you're swearing
You're not sorry
For teaching me
How to come

Soul Painting

When you snap
Your fingers.
You know that
Poets respond more
When the audience
Is snapping their fingers.
And you were
Ready to choke me
Until I tapped out,
My pouting made you
Try to re-teach me
My ABC's because
Please,
I was brain damaged
When you left me
Speechless and screaming
From fulfilling your needs.
When the stop sign
On my heart bled
From all the words
You never said,
Like "I love you,"
It spilled a
Wine red from the pain.
You wanted to stain me
Like a wooden bench
You could lie on
When something
More comfortable
Was already taken.
I've always been second
To your affection
And after a few seconds,
My arms can't stop
Shaking.
I go breaking

Into your home life
With a knife at my neck,
As if I was a sacrifice
Any god would care
To take or
You would care
To lose.
But there was
A bruise wrapped
Around my eye,
Black as the night
You first screwed me
And told me
I wasn't pretty.
I wasn't the best
You'd ever had
Because "Bad sex" is
My new nickname.
And sure,
You smooth talked
Your way between
My legs,
Slurring your words
Like 2 kegs of beer
Could make me
Any more attractive.
And you sweet-talked
Your way out of them,
Like I was a sin
And mistakes weren't made
For saints like you.
I was the problem,
And you weren't
The solution,
No matter how many
Times I made you try

Soul Painting

To fit inside my
Messed up body.
You were getting sucked
In like a guilt trip
Buckling at your knees,
And I seized the opportunity
To kiss you.
I should've
Let you fall
Like a shooting star
Across my chest,
Landing in the galaxy
Of scars on my rib cage
That keep in the
Broken promises
And lost love notes,
And keep out stormy nights
And fights that leave me
Bruised up from
A low punch in the gut.
I let you unlock me,
Dig your hands into me,
And get bloody fingers
From my glassy insides.
I let you go down on me
And then leave because
I wasn't the right
Woman to be with
When morning came
The sun was to blame
For your shamed hands
And my shirt on your floor.
I knew you'd hurt me,
And I knew you'd break me
Like a tape recorder,
Unraveling in your hands.

The contents of which
Kept skipping over
Every other word besides
"Pathetic, Pathetic, Pa-Pa-"
Please let me breathe.
You retrained my throat
To gasp for air
And not care
What the hell
Would happen
To my lungs
If I stopped swallowing
Your bitter lies
And choking back
Empty cries for help
In the night.
I never should've let you
Inside when you came
Knocking at my confidence.
But I let you in
And taught you to
Kiss me until I was
Dragged down
In your fisting me
Every time you grinned,
Because you couldn't
Find pleasure
In just loving me.

Side Effects
a Poem For Monica Lewinsky

Rock me back and forth,
Cradle me in your branches,
Kiss my high horse goodbye for me.
Hold me down as I inject
Daily doses of reality into my bloodstream.
Because shooting up is better than being
Shot down by a man who carries
His self-medicated soliloquys
Like track marks on his tongue.
White walls are crooking their necks sideways
To hear the juicy stories of my
Ex-lover and me.
I bite at my wrist with dulled teeth,
When other girls decorate their wrists
With corsages and bracelets.
They say I have this need to
Mutilate the exterior to make it
Match my inferior interior,
But I know that mirrors would
Shatter before reflecting my
Appearance- a shadow of a ghost,
The emptiest half of emptiness.
You left me after learning my red lines
Were edits improving the imperfection of my skin,
Like your latest political propaganda:
Flesh eating itself,
Peeling like apples back from my core.
I purse 2 lips to the cigarette
Like a death kiss,
A wish to put Sleeping Beauty
Back in bed,

But these are my side effects
To the medication I
Abused for years.
There are scars circling around veins,
Tangoing for my life or death.
Date rape drug me until I can't feel
You remove my bleeding heart,
Red as the popped cherry stem you tied
Between my legs.
I will keep medicating myself
With the memories of you,
Bleed them out like an exorcism
Of the ghost you left within me.
I hear it calling my name
With disgust.
It reminds me of how much
I missed the smell of your cologne-
1 part misogyny, 5 parts retaliation
For your political fiascos.
Lay me down gently,
Turn me on my side,
Until I feel the effects.
Caress me, and don't forget to thank me
With a spanking and your tip
When you sneak out at night from your shame.
Morning came like you—too soon.
Tell the presses that you don't know me,
"I did not have sexual relations with this woman."
But remember I'm more than the prostitute,
More than the sexy former intern,
Behind this 2 way mirror- glassy eyes
Shattering from witnessing myself
As the sexual tapes you didn't
Bet your wife on, an affair for the
Internal parts of your body,

Soul Painting

A lie for the external.
I guess we both have to self-medicate sometimes,
But I was mad all along,
You thrust
Hot and heavy,
Into me,
Wikileaking your information
Inside of me,
Like I leaked our story to the masses.
The sanity is slipping away
Into the six white walls,
Orange jacket,
Me.
I knew my side effects,
And I'm glad to see you've joined me here.
Looks like you've caught the madness, too.
Here, they call it Truth.
Rock me like a baby in your branches,
Maybe we will both fall when
November comes.

No Vacancy

My head and my heart keep hurdling over hope, trying not to kick down reality, and her sweet whisper keeps knocking on the doors of my eardrums, screaming "let me in let me in" but the graveyard that is known as my skin says "no vacancy. Find a new place to stay, to slay the beasts of self-confidence and determination." I'm living in a nation without pain, but the main lie comes from the bones rattling in my chest, from a bullet that is his name. Poet. Not good enough yet. Poet. Too young to be told ready, set, engaged. Poet. The man who took away my breath, leaving a gaping hole in my heart, and a part of me evaporated the day he flew away with his other princess. And I keep running, like a soldier, head first into battle, waiting for the spears and the guns to plunge straight for all of my insecurities. Maybe carpe diem was only really meant for Caesar's army, but I want to be on the front lines, fighting against the sickening sweet breath of self hatred, fighting against the alcoholic beverages that call my underage name, fighting against the pain of wanting to slice 19 years into as many parts as the red tally marks on my wrist. I'm just a child, they say, as they squeeze my small hand a little tighter, walking me across the street that separates poet from writer, and I swear, I'm not just a fighter, I'm a warrior. I will be jumping hurdles all my life. I'll be stumbling like a drunk over my words every time I see your face. Your smile still nauseates me, and I wish I could rip your smug little grin from your face, instead of seeing your sad eyes lying to me once more. You're beautiful, they whisper, but it's a lie.

Soul Painting

You're smart, they whisper, but only because I guard my thighs like a prized possession. You're not her, they whisper, and that last part resonates through every part of my hollow body until I start feeling ill. And I'm sick of running. My fingers are tired from tracing the life lines on my palms, all of which stop at the same point: the day I met you. And my defibrillator hasn't worked yet, so I'm still on life support, running on the report that you might not hate me as much as you said, and your voice is the only medicine I need, but I refuse to take it and you refuse to give it, so I'm not running anymore. The core of my soul is so rotten from the poor excuse that is me. I want to know what it is to be free from this sickening sweet voice banging on the door of my eardrums. "Let me in let me in" it's still screaming. I check to see if I'm dreaming, and then crack open the door to let the floods of the Red Sea pour in one last time. There was no vacancy.

Black Holes

I chart the constellations
Of freckles on your face,
Calling them miracles
Instead of mess ups.
You're a solar system of possibilities
And I'm your star catcher,
But it's my job to
Watch you fall apart,
Piece by piece into the darkness
Of your depression,
Until the black hole
Starts to suck us both inside.
I wanted to pull away,
Hang onto the rope
At the edge of the cliff,
And I would've made it
Out of your destruction,
Tugging and pulling
And breaking apart
Like the threads of
An infinite and infinitesimal
Universe collapsing,
I would have been your survivor,
Had I not been...

...Pushed.

Soul Painting

Part 5

Soul Painting

"I put my heart and my soul
into my work, and have lost
my mind in the process."

-Vincent Van Gogh

Soul Painting

Jocelyn Mosman

Why I Write

I used to write poetry
About peace and nature,
And my soliloquy was
The beauty of the earth
And the magnificence of love.
I wish I could write poetry
Like that again,
But now, the pen
Has become my sword,
Paper my shield,
Like a defense mechanism
When I'm under attack.
But I don't want war.
I want to create,
Not destruct.
I want to oppose,
Not conform.
I'm not wanting
To write
Just to put
Others down.
I want to find
Peace inside words,
Like a hiding place
In my closet where
I keep my journals.
I want to write as a reminder,
Remember those who loved me
And those who I loved.
I am writing
To create Band-Aids

Soul Painting

Over the gaping wounds,
To heal my broken bones
With a cast of characters
And pretty phrases.
I want to notice
How green grass is
And how rain feels
On dried up skin.
I want to write poetry,
Not death certificates
To ex-lovers and ex-friends,
Because losing a friend
Is worse than losing battles.
I'm not fighting
By writing my soul music.
I am putting down my sword,
Watching it shine in the moonlight.
I am paper mâché-ing blank pages
Onto my skin
So you can't see the scars
Bleeding through.
I want to write poetry
That sounds like
Starting over,
Because endings are too final
And beginnings are too short.
I want to blossom
Like flowers on rainy days.
I'm thirsty for good poetry,
And I want to write it out
Until my heart doesn't know
The difference between
Poetry and dreaming.
I've always been a dreamer.

And I'll keep writing
Until my pen runs out of ink,
Until the black stains on my hands
Reflect the night sky,
Covered in little white stars.
I used to write poetry
About peace and nature,
And I want to keep writing,
Not fighting for a name,
Not blaming anyone but myself,
Just writing the truth,
Until that peace comes back.

Sailors' Knot

The ropes that tied the noose
Also tied the knot
In our love affair.
We were sailors shipwrecking
Ourselves on deserted islands
Looking for a love that lasted
Past the light brigade
Of lighthouses and dark alleyways.
We were marooned, you said.
But I preferred to imagine
We were magenta'ed, I said.
My colors never quite matched yours.
You were an ocean of flaws
And I was a sea of possibilities,
Getting lost in the life boat
That led me far away from you.
The ropes are a little looser now
But I can feel the burn around my neck
Where you used to kiss me goodnight
And the burn around my cheeks
Where tearstains remind me
Of the rivers of lies
Separating us from our sailor's knot
Another fight for love.

Jocelyn Mosman

Spiderweb Kisses

We met in the shadows,
Silhouettes touching on pavement,
A dance of movement
That only exists in sunlight.
Our shadows had voices.
By day, our shadows flirted
With spiderweb kisses,
Weaving like fingers intertwining
From a distance.
The world dimmed down
Like a touch lamp
Every time our shadows met.
But in the darkness,
There were no touching shadows.
Only your darkness
Crawling beneath my flesh
Until my shadows and yours
Met inside my eardrums.
Our shadows had voices.
At night, our shadows screamed
That I'd never be strong enough
To reach past our shadows
In the daylight and slip
My hand into yours.

Symphony

My heart is a symphony played on broken strings, a violin screeching its lonely sonata to the moonlight, and the beating of blood into veins is a sight for sore eyes as my heart beats for the man who beat me until my thighs bled for mercy. It was a decrescendo into falling on my knees pleading for forgiveness, begging, weeping, praying for The Lord to steal the tear ducts from my eyes so I would never be able to cry again. My wrists marked the five red lines of staff where I transcribed the notes that my screams made when he broke me like piccolo every time he hurt me. Sixteenth notes created track marks on my arms from where he made me breathe faster and faster and faster and faster and... Rest. His fists were glissandos on harp strings, leaving scales on my body to remind me of a time when the world was a roller coaster, going up and down. His eyes were cellos, smooth and deep, playing haunting memories in the soundtracks of my mind, only to find the recordings buried deep in the caverns of my ribcage. And they are playing like a broken record, playing like a broken record, playing like a broken record, and for the record, it's playing our love song, trying to sew up every wrong note in its harmony but only untying heart strings with the verses singing love me do love me do love me don't... Stop singing me to sleep every night. Stop waiting for the sight of me to make you find respite in the twilight of our youth. Stop. Wait for the coda. There won't be a dry eye in the audience of the performance hall of my cells racing through my body. The broken violin has been pacing itself this whole performance and the strings have ripped themselves in half. There's blood on the floor. My heart is a symphony, and the piano just ended its final note. Black and ivory make me fall to my knees, head bowed, eyes to the ground, like an execution. The low C is the firing squad that lands the bullets one, two, three, counting out the fingering, in my bare chest. The rest is one of triumph and one of pain. Perspiring like a musician who has worked a lifetime for his name, his fingers fall from the keys like his hand fell from the trigger that shattered the glass reflecting the beautiful silence of music ringing in my ears. The drums in my ears keep beating, and my heart is pounding and resounding out the notes of the words he once said "Passion Over Everything." Silence fell like a red curtain, draping over my insecurities. Our thighs slapped together like applause.

Stringing

I was stringing

My way along,

Chalking myself up

In white lace,

Bow tied

Tight to the melody.

I only wanted harmony

But I let the cello

Bridge my way

Across new waters,

Never turning back

To watch the

Burning of

My past.

Starry, Starry Nights

I wanted to see the universe
And you showed me
A telescope and told me
To look for you when
I was away.
The moon is always the same
Wherever we are
And however far we are apart.
But you forgot about the nights
That the skies are black
And the moon is behind
The cloud cover.
So I uncovered
My empty sky chest
And drew stars
In red ink.
I let them sink
Into burning my heart
And let the black hole
Inside me
Make the existence
Of you collapse for a while.
My style has always been
Wishing on shooting stars,
Because forget the galaxies
Already carved on
My Milky Way chest.
I've been
Drizzling like caramel
And sticking to my tongue
Like my scars couldn't be

Soul Painting

Removed from the roof
Of my mouth.
I want to follow the stars
South into your arms,
But they were never aligned
For our fates.
I could only create new stars
In my galaxy
Because the ones I saw
In your eyes were dull
And fading after
Long distance became
Light years away from
Being together again.
I couldn't think of you
And draw them
Because you always seemed
Too universally important
For me to trade your
Starry starry nights
For my Van Gogh
Moments of going
Into my dark places
And empty spaces
And being consumed
By the gravity
Pulling me back
To old flames
On older stars.
You were always a
Wish away
And a shooting star
From me

Going crazy
In the distance.
You were my first star
Every night.
And you shine bright
Even in my darkness.
You teach me to look
Into your telescope,
Search the skies for any sign
Of our matching astrological
Symbol.
Burn me up inside
And I'll be just fine
Looking into
Your beautiful, beautiful eyes.

Soul Painting

I brush my soul on new canvas,
A stroke of pain-
Purple as a butterfly's broken wing,
A stroke of beauty-
Blue as the night skies in August,
A stroke of strength-
Brown as the dirt that covers our sunburnt skin,
A stroke of confidence-
Orange as an October sunset,
A stroke of femininity-
Pink as the blush that bepainted Juliet's maiden cheeks,
A stroke of envy-
Green as his earthy eyes,
A stroke of weakness-
Red as the sun's rays on her wrists,
Painting a picture of a woman
On white, white canvas-
Innocence turned into a rainbow
Of understanding and youth.
My soul paints the colors of truth,
And the day falls away into the shadows
Of large strokes of guilt-
Black as the coffee beans brewed
In basements of sin.

Epilogue

Jocelyn Mosman

about the **A**uthor

Jocelyn Mosman is 19 years old and attends Mount Holyoke College in South Hadley, Massachusetts. Outside of poetry, she is majoring in English and Politics. She is a Pre-Law student with experience in family and criminal law. She plans to attend Law School, and then pursue a career in international Human Rights Law, working with the United Nations.

This is Mosman's second poetry book, following *Soul Music,* which was released March 2013. She has been published in multiple anthologies, including Unitarian Universalist Church of Midland's *Solice* and *Interlude*, Permian Basin Chapter, Poetry Society of Texas *Wind, Sand, and Sky*, Brian Wrixon's *Summer Poetry*, and several national anthologies, including Creative Communication's *A Celebration of Poets*, The American Library of Poetry's *Gifted,* and Poetry.com's *Immortal Verses*. In addition to her publication in anthologies, she also recently published an anthology, featuring 16 poets from West Texas, entitled *We Are The 500*.

Mosman has also been published in *Rogue Particles Magazine, Cum Laude Weekly, Drunk Monkeys, Decanto Publications, Teen Ink, Red Fez, Crack the Spine,* and *Silver Birch Press.*

Mosman is the founder of West Texas Poets. She is also a member of the Conscious Poets Society, the Poetry Society of Texas, and Northampton Poetry. She was President of the Permian Basin Chapter, Poetry Society of Texas from 2013-2014.

Mosman has performed at various venues across West Texas and Massachusetts. A few of her spoken word awards include first place at a poetry slam in June 2013, third place at a haiku head to head in January 2014, cash prize poetry slam winner in March 2014, host and opening performer at Mary Lambert's concert in February 2014, and Poetry Jam participant and opening performer for Striver's Row poets Miles Hodges and Alysia Harris in October 2013.

After a decade of writing poetry, Mosman has formulated a family of poets that stretch from Massachusetts to India to Europe to Texas. She is hoping to release a spoken word album within the next year of her poetry being performed. Poetry is not always meant to be read, but is always meant to be felt.

Acknowledgments

Grateful acknowledgment is made to the following journals, in which these poems originally appeared, sometimes in slightly different form

Crack the Spine: "D"
Teen Ink: "Bus B43"
West Texas Poets'
We Are The 500 : "D," "Push Me"

Special Thanks

To my parents, Jim and Jennifer Mosman, for always being supportive of me, even if you did not always understand why it was so important to me.

To Jessica, Jon, and Taylor Grondin, for believing in me and always being a listening ear.

To Katharina Ibsen and Lisa Engel, for being my German sisters and listening to my secrets.

To Ann and Ed Mosman, and Jan Stein, for keeping an interest in my writing, even through my "experimental" periods.

To William Stein, for giving me all the tools I need to keep you alive with every verse I write.

To Jelene Ballard, for being the teacher who told me I could do it. One day I hope to be as much of an inspiration as you are every day.

To Teresa Gazella, for helping me gain confidence in my writing.

To Aaron Cox and Susie Haynes, for being more than just debate coaches, but also life coaches and friends.

To Robert Shaw, for keeping me humble about my writing and pushing me further than I thought possible.

To David McCann, for teaching me the ancient art of sijo.

To Tobi Cogswell, for your kindness and your advice.

To Loretta Diane Walker, for teaching me at a young age the beauty of music and of poetry.

To Kat Copeland, for giving me the chance to reignite the poetry flame in West Texas.

To Tony Henninger, for being kind enough to present me with this unique and wonderful opportunity.

To Melissa May-Dunn, for taking the time to write out a review for me, even if we are only Facebook friends. Also, for being such a beautiful inspiration to women everywhere.

To Ryan Austin Fryoux, for the cover photographs, and for being a rule breaker.

To Dalyn Spurgeon, for being my Haiku Goddess and muse.

To Shermila Kher, Alyssa Carter, and Kimberly Cash, for being my best friends and sisters, no matter where we end up in this world.

To Selena Cardona, for listening to way too many of pre-slam poetry rehearsals.

To West Texas Poets, for being my non-biological family.

To Northampton Poetry and Conscious Poets Society, for being my long-distance non-biological family.

To S.M., for allowing me to share your story.

To M.R., T.D., D.C.R., J.N., for being muses in your own special way, even if you never knew that you were.

To you, dear readers, for making this process infinitely more special.

To Inner Child Press, Ltd., for being so wonderful to me throughout this process and for making my dreams come true.

Web Links to Jocelyn

Facebook
www.facebook.com/SeraphineThePoet

Tumblr
www.seraphinethepoet.tumblr.com

Twitter
www.twitter.com/PoetSera

Instagram
www.instagram.com/PoetSera

Email
jmosman7@aol.com

Inner Child Press

Inner Child Press is a Publishing Company Founded and Operated by Writers. Our personal publishing experiences provides us an intimate understanding of the sometimes daunting challenges Writers, New and Seasoned may face in the Business of Publishing and Marketing their Creative "Written Work".

For more Information

Inner Child Press

www.innerchildpress.com

intouch@innerchildpress.com

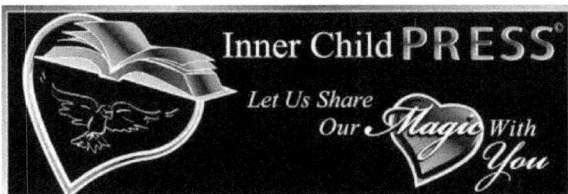

www.ingramcontent.com/pod-product-compliance
Lightning Source LLC
LaVergne TN
LVHW021538080426
835509LV00019B/2702